Marriage License Bonds
of
Accomack County, Virginia

From 1774 to 1806

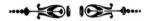

Listed and Indexed By

Stratton Nottingham

97-1325

CLEARFIELD

Reprinted for
Clearfield Company, Inc. by
Genealogical Publishing Co., Inc.
Baltimore, Maryland
1991, 1994, 1997

Originally published: Onancock, Virginia, 1927
Reprinted: Genealogical Publishing Co., Inc.
Baltimore, 1965, 1978
Library of Congress Catalogue Card Number 65-26465
International Standard Book Number 0-8063-0263-1
Made in the United States of America

Abbott, John m. Bridget Barnes, dau. Susanna
    Barnes, 16 Jan. 1775 William Black Bunting
    sur.

Abbott, John m. Leah Abbott, 10 Dec. 1785, Thomas
    Parker sur.

Adams, David m. Comfort Ewell, 21 Jan. 1806, Obed
    Adams sur.

Adams, Obid m. Sally Silverthorn, 5 Nov. 1798,
    Robert Taylor sur.

Adams, Stephen m. Betsy Lurton, 27 Aug. 1798,
    Thomas Jenkins sur.

Addison, John m. Susanna Kellam, 10 Oct. 1786,
William Leatherbury sur.

Addison, Levi m. Dority Aimes, 22 Dec. 1800, Benj.
    Aimes sur.

Addison, William m. Nancy Milby, wid. John Milby
    23 Aug. 1806, Shadrack Ames sur.

Ague, William m. Susey James 10 Jan. 1801

Ailworth, William m. Nancy Duncan, 2 Sept. 1805,
    Major Bird sur.

Aimes (Ames), Benjamin m. Betsy Rayfield, 6 Jan. 1801
    Thomas Scarburgh sur.

Aimes, Joseph m. Tinney Snead, 19 Oct. 1795

Aimes, John m. Phillis Garrison, 4 Oct. 1786,
    Littleton Addison sur.

Aimes, Richard m. Leah Seymour, 30 Aug. 1802

Aimes, Thomas m. Sukey Wise, 31 Mar. 1794

Aires (Ayres), Francis, m. Margaret Rodgers, 27
    Oct. 1785, Laban Chandler sur.

Aires, Thomas m. Betty Chandler, 8 Sept. 1787,
    John Custis sur.

Allen, Joseph m. Rachel Dickerson, 27 Dec. 1791

Allen, Joseph m. Hannah Hutson, 2 June 1794

Allen, John m. Margaret Arbuckle, 11 Nov. 1785
    Edward Arbuckle sur.

Ames (Aimes) Benjamin m. Nancy Hyslop, 21 Oct. 1805
    John Ames sur.

Ames, Levin m. Comfort Scott, 30 Dec. 1805, Richard
    Bloxom sur.

Andrews, Jacob m. Anne Porter, 16 Dec. 1801, William
    Andrews sur.

Ardis, Daniel m. Tabitha Mason, 10 Nov. 1798

Arlington, John m. Rosey Bagwell, 5 April 1785
    William Mears sur.

Ashby, James m. Matilda Custis, 23 June 1794

Ashby, William m. Polly Shield, 2 Oct. 1804, Ismy
    Shield sur.

Augustus, William, free negro, m. Sary Davis, free
    negro, 27 Jan. 1806, Isaac Holland sur.

Ayres (Aires), Levin m. Sinah Baker, 3 Dec. 1805,
    Ezekiel Baker sur.

Ayres, William m. Rachel Justice, 18 Jan. 1786, John
    Riggs sur.

Badger, John m. Sally Underhill, 1 Aug. 1798, John
    Edmunds sur.

Bagwell, Charles m. Nancy Grinalds, 25 Jan. 1791

Bagwell, George P. m. Peggy Dix, 5 June 1797

Bagwell, Isacah m. Christina Newton, 2 Jan. 1790

Bagwell, John m. Anne Young, 25 Jan. 1786, Edmund
    Scarbrough sur.

Baines, John m. Nancy Baines, 1 Sept. 1790

Baker, Daniel m. Peggy Copes 31 July 1804, James
    White sur.

Baker, Ezekiel m. Nancy Ganet, 30 September 1799

Baker, Hezekiah m. Jamimah Hannaford, 25 May 1787,
    William Gibb sur.

Baker, Shadrack m. Nancy Sterling, 10 Jan. 1798

Baker, Stephen m. Hepsy Baker, 22 Feb. 1802,
    Solomon Baker sur.

Bandy, Kendall m. Rosey Bunting, 26 Oct. 1799, Mark
    Ewell sur.

Bandy, Kendall m. Rachel Penn, 5 July 1804, James
    Morris sur.

Barnes, John m. Susanna Lillaston, wid. Jacob
    Lillaston, 12 July 1806

Barnes, Spencer m. Margaret Hinnman (About 1798 -
    Badly damaged)

Barnes, Samuel m. Nancy Doe, 24 Jan. 1804, Isaac
    Dix sur.

Bayly, Esme m. Elizabeth d. Kellam, 30 Dec. 1805,
    George Kellam sur.

Bayly, John m. Esther Bradford, 21 Jan. 1775, Edmund
    Bayly sur.

Bayly, Levin m. Hepsey Cord, 6 Feb. 1799, Thomas
    Bayly sur.

Bayly, Thomas M. m. Margaret Pettitt Cropper, dau.
    John Cropper, Jr., 31 Mar. 1802, Edmund Bayly
    sur.

Bayly, Zadock m. Nelly Lucas, 13 Jan. 1790

Beasy, Micajah m. Betsey Warrington, 26 Aug. 1805,
    Skinner Marshall sur.

Beavans, Walter m. Hannah Peck, 2 July 1804, Mathias
    Outten sur.

Beavans, William m. Martha Brodwater, 9 July 1790

Beavans, William H. m. Betsy M. Core, 8 Feb. 1800,
    George P. Bagwell sur.

Becket, Peter m. Ariena Nutt, dau. Adah Nutt, 10
    Jan. 1800, Babel Major sur.

Beesly, Smith m. Betty Bennett -- June 1795, James
    Carmine sur. (Badly damaged)

Beech, Ezekiel m. Anne Spiers, 26 Nov. 1785, John
    Spiers sur.

Belote, Caleb m. Euphamy Edwards, 26 Aug. 1805,
    Zerobabel Edwards sur.

Belote, George m. Peggy Michom, 1 Jan. 1802, John
    Savage of Abel sur.

Belote, John m. Sarah Hawley, 14 May 1800, John
    Savage sur.

Belote, John m. Rachel Mears, 11 May 1800, John
    Savage sur.

Belote, John, Jr. m. Sally Mears, 15 Dec. 1801,
    William Heath sur.

Belotte, Noah m. Elizabeth Wise, 2 Feb. 1775, John
    Wise sur.

Bell, Edward m. Nancy Guy, 6 Apr. 1806, William Budd
    sur.

Bell, William m. Rachel Bradford, 3 Oct. 1800, John
    Bell sur.

Bell, William m. Nicey Kelley, 13 Jan. 1800, Levi
    Small sur.

Bennett, James m. Sally Garret, 24 Jan. 1798

Benson, Jonah m. Betsy Core, 17 June 1794

Benson, Joseph m. Ann Warrington, dau. Teakle &
    Ester Warrington, 23 Aug. 1805, Southy
    Warrington sur.

Benston, Daniel m. Betsy Taylor, 26 Sept. 1800,
    Isaac Duncan sur.

Benston, John m. Polly White, Wid. 9 Oct. 1801,
    John Turner sur.

Benston, McKenney m. Vianna Kelley, 29 Sept. 1801,
Benston, Zadock m. Nancy Taylor, 8 Dec. 1789
Bibbins, Thomas m. Arena Becket, 2 Aug. 1800, Peter
     Bibbins sur.
Bird, Ebern m. Peggy Bunting, 3 Jan. 1801, Jacob Bird
     sur.
Bird, John m. Esther Ross, 7 June 1790, William
     S--------- sur.
Bird, Johannes m. Peggy Kelly, 10 Sept. 1802
Bird, Parker m. Keziah Gilaspee, 4 Feb. 1800, Ezekiel
     Bloxom sur.
Bird, William m. Caziah Hinman, 7 Jan. 1792
Blades, Jesse m. Nelly Grey, 5 Dec. 1786, Thomas Guy
     sur.
Blake, William m. Rachel Taylor, 11 Feb. 1788
Bloxom, Argil m. Lucretia Evans, 28 Sept. 1795
Blosom, Ezekiel m. Sally Wimbrough, 27 Dec. 1798,
     Thomas Justice sur.
Bloxom, James m. Molly Hinman, 10 Jan. 1807, William
     Davis sur.
Bloxom, Major m. Betsey Hope, 10 F b. 1799
Bloxom, Nicholas m. Nancy Holloway, 8 Dec. 1798,
     William Stephens sur.
Bloxom, Robert m. Nanny Belote, 10 Mar. 1787,
     Handcock Belote sur.
Bloxom, Richard m. Betsy Giddens, 3 Nov. 1801
Bloxom, Richard, Sr. m. Jinney Fletcher, 29 July
     1805, Richard Bloxom, Jr. sur.
Bloxsom, Severn m. Catherine Kellam, 24 Feb. 1794
     (Badly damaged)
Blosom, Simpsn, Jr. m. Tabitha Bull, 29 Oct. 1799
Bloxum, Southy m. Susanna Kellum, 5 May 1804, John
     Abbott Bundick sur.
Bloxom, Woodman m. Nancy Matthews, 8 Jan. 1798
Boggs, Francis m. Agnes Crowson, 4 Mar. 1802,
     Joseph Boggs sur.
Boisnard, John m. Sarah Teackle, 25 Apr. 1783,
     William Gibb sur.
Bonewell, George m. Bridget Bull, 14 Sept. 1789,
     Isaiah Evans sur.
Bonwell, George m. Polly Rodgers, 17 Dec. 1800,
     George Salisbury, sur.
Bonwell, John (of Dolly) m. Catherine Kellam, 26
     Apr. 1806, Thomas Snead sur.

Bonewell, Southy m. Mary Snead, 27 Mar. 1787, Skinner
    Wallop sur.

Bonwell, Stephen m. Peggy Topping, 21 May 1796,
    George Topping sur.

Booth, John m. Esther Birch, 9 Jan. 1801, John Burch
    sur.

Booth, Joseph m. Martha Spalding, 25 July 1797

Bowdoin, Edward m. Elizabeth Bloxom, 11 Feb. 1797

Bowdin, William m. Anne Hickman, 25 Mar. 1805

Brockshaw, Jacob m. Levinear Evans dau. Richard
    Evans, 30 July 1800, Severn Tyler sur.

Bradford, Jacob m. Margaret Bell, 29 Apr. 1806,
    Benston Bradford sur.

Bradford, Littleton m. Nancy Harmon, 2 Feb. 1802,
    William Elliott sur.

Bradford, Thomas m. Alesy P. Bradford, 12 Oct. 1786,
    George Hyslop sur.

Brewington, William m. Mary Waterfield, 10 Mar. 1805

Brimer, Caleb m. Rachel Marriner, 3 July 1800,
    Stephen Bloxom sur.

Brimer, Joseph m. Betsy Willett, 15 Dec. 1801, George
    Willett sur.

Brittingham, Levi m. Polly Holt, 10 Feb. 1802, John
    Holt sur.

Brown, William, free negro, m. Nancy Griffin, free
    negro, 27 Dec. 1804, Levin Godfree sur.

Brown, William m. Silvia Mathews, 9 Mar. 1801, Levin
    Godfry sur.

Brown, William, free negro, m. Jenney, free negro
    6 July 1802

Broadwater, Edward m. Polly Case, 30 Nov. 1799,
    David Mills sur.

Broadwater, Henry m. Sophia R. Powell, 12 Apr. 1802,
    Jacob Burton sur.

Broadwater, Joseph m. Sarah Broadwater, 26 Jan. 1790

Broadwater, Jacob m. Mary James, 5 Oct. 1789

Broadwater, Southy m. Esther Hill, 19 Oct. 1791 .

Broadwater, Southy m. Atta Broadwater, 29 Dec. 1806,
    Major Hinman sur.

Broadwater, Savage m. Nancy Broadwater, 28 Apr. 1806,
    David Miles sur.

Budd, William m. Betsy Young, 13 Apr. 1802, Robinson
    Scott sur.

Budd, William m. Betsey Parker, 10 June 1806

Bull, Daniel m. Betty Giddens, 25 Nov. 1789 (Badly
      Damaged)
Bull, Eli m. Nancy Fitzgerald, 24 Dec. 1785, Elijah
      Fitzgerald sur.
Bull, Ezekiel m. Susanna Colloney, 25 Feb. 1796
Bull, John m. Sarah Russell, 29 July 1774, Preeson
      Snead sur.
Bull, John, Jr. m. Nancy Turnell, 30 Jan. 1796
Bull, Richard m. Caty Hargis, 13 June 1806
Bull, Southy m. Susanna Fitzgerald, 7 July 1785,
      Charles Snead sur.
Bull, William m. Nancy Drummond, 20 Sept. 1799,
      Thorowgood Bell sur.
Bunting, George m. Sally Ramsay, wid. 26 Sept. 1806
      George W. Burton sur.
Bunting, Smith m. Nanny Rodgers, 5 Dec. 1805, John
      Phillips sur.
Bunting, Thomas m. Susanna Bayley, 22 Dec. 1785,
      Jonathan Bunting sur.
Bunting, Thomas m. Rose Evans - (About 1800 -
      Badly damaged)
Bunting, William Black m. Sally Cropper, 15 Sept.
      1785, Preeson Snead sur.
Bundick, Abbott m. Betsy Taylor, 11 Sept. 1791,
      Isaac Taylor sur.
Bundick, George m. Betty Laws, 25 Aug. 1785, Caleb
      Broadwater sur.
Bundick, George m. Rachel Mason, 23 Mar. 1802,
      George Taylor sur.
Bundick, John m. Sally Nock, 27 Dec. 1798, William
      Baker sur.
Bundick, James m. Nancy Selby, 23 Dec. 1806, Mack
      Crippen sur.
Bundick, Richard m. Lany Nelson, 4 Dec. 1804
Burchett, John m. Scarburgh Northam, 2 July 1789
Burdett, Thomas m. Tabitha Wallop, 20 Jan. 1792

Cammell, John m. Leah Davis, 28 Jan. 1799, Nehemiah
      Bratton sur.
Carss, John m. Elizabeth Stakes, 16 Feb. 1790
Carmine, James m. Dinah Bennett, 17 Mar. 1795,
      John Bradford sur.
Carlile, Alexander m. Milly Parker, 19 Feb. 1785,
      Jacob Savage sur.

Carpenter, Jacob m. Elizabeth Holloway 13------
      1805, James Conner sur. (Badly damaged)

Casey, Patrick m. Charity Smith, 7 Mar. 1786, William
      Smith sur.

Case, Major m. Betsy Riggs, 12 Jan. 1799, Jacob
      Andrews sur.

Charles, freed by Drummond, m. Elizabeth Stevens,
      free negro, 24 July 1806

Chapman, William m. Jane Evans, 27 Apr. 1802, Charles
      Stockly sur.

Charnock, Abel m. Atha Turner, 10 June 1786, William
      Gibb sur.

Chambers, Edmund m. Mary Wise, 5 June 1785, Keily
      Wise sur.

Chambers, Elijah m. Peggy Melson, 8 Feb. 1786, Rufus
      Huntley sur.

Chambers, Major m. Elizabeth Guy, 23 May 1784,
      William Leatherbury sur.

Chandler, Elisha m. Amy Chandler, 7 Aug. 1805,
      Mitchell Chandler sur.

Chandler, James m. Peggy Burton Phillips, 25 Nov.
      1801

Chandler, Mitchell m. Keziah Laylor, 3 May 1802,
      Arthur Laylor sur.

Chandler, William m. Phamey Ironmonger, 5 May 1801,
      Edward Ironmonger sur.

Cheshire, Eli m. Anne Chace, 14 Oct. 1806, Ephraim
      Outten sur.

Chesher, Ephraim m. Lusey Marshall, 13 Oct. 1798,
      George Wilson sur.

Cheshire, Purnell m. Lane Trader, 21 Sept. 1804,
      Shadrack Warrington sur.

Cheshire, Thomas m. Susan Moore, dau. Bratcher
      Moore, 14 Aug. 1806, Jacob Andrews sur.

Chisher, William m. Leah Marshall, 7 Aug. 1797

Christopher, George m. Susanna Fisher, 29 June 1795,

Christopher, Williamson m. Leah Wilson, 4 June 1789

Churn, William m. Nancy Harrison, 24 Dec. 1791

Clayton, Dennis m. Susanna Riley, 12 Feb. 1800,
      Charles Bagwell sur.

Coard, Parker, M. Polly Abbott, 23 June 1806, George
      Thomas sur.

Coke, Richard m. Laney Taylor, 11 Jan. 1792

Coleburn, James m. Sally Taylor, 28 Apr. 1791

Coleburn, Revel m. Peggy Polk, 7 Sept. 1785, William
        Polk sur.

Collins, George m. Polly Wise, 28 Dec. 1791

Collins, James m. Fanney Marshall, wid. 16 Mar.1801,
        William Johnson sur.

Collins, John m. Sally Thornton, 12 Aug. 1799, John
        Watson sur.

Collins, John m. Mrs. Polly Lamberson, 31 Dec. 1801,
        Elias Taylor sur.

Collings, John m. Diadamia Cherix, dau. Jesse
        Cherix, 5 Sept. 1806, George Marshall sur.

Collins, Skinner m. Rebecca Taylor, 21 July 1806,
        George Marshall sur.

Collins, William m. Molly Benston, 30 Jan. 1788

Collins, William m. Rebecca Owen, 17 Aug. 1788

Colony, Elijah m. Sarah Evans, 23 Aug. 1792

Coloney, George m. Sarah Walker, 7 Dec. 1798, Robert
        Davis sur.

Colny, James m. Elizabeth Stephens, 22 Feb. 1806

Colony, John m. Elizabeth Smith, 22 Dec. 1774,
        William Colony sur.

Colony, Kendall m. Tabitha Right, 23 Jan. 1796

Colony, Upshur m. Anne Darby, 7 Mar. 1775, John
        Colony sur.

Colony, Watson m. Rosey Bayly, 18 Feb. 1806, Walter
        Mears sur.

Colony, William m. Elizabeth Watson, 11 Feb. 1795,
        Robert Twiford sec.

Connoway, William m. Elizabeth Reid, 3 Feb. 1786,
        Levin Rodgers sec.

Conquest, William m. Nancy Drummond, 3 Jan. 1797

Copes, Levin m. Salley Metcalf, 12 Sept. 1787,
        Southy Simpson sur.

Copes, Parker m. Tabitha Edmunds, 4 Oct. 1787,
        Levin Copes sur.

Copes, Southy m. Euphamy Ironmonger, 2 May 1785,
        Southy Simpson sur.

Copeland, Lemuel m. Anna Hall, 12 Jan. 1801

Corbin, George m. Nancy Sterling, 17 Sept. 1796

Costin, Ezekiel m. Sinah Clemmons, 8 Aug. 1785,
        Bennett Mason sur.

Cotton, William m. Salley Garrett, 8 Dec. 1798,
        William Pettitt sur.

Cox, James m. Elizabeth Wise Bayly, 25 June, 1774,
        James Broughton sur.

Crippen, Samuel m. Elizabeth Wise, 8 Apr. 1806, John
    Wise, Jr. sur.
Crippin, Thomas m. Susanna Custis, 6 Sept. 1783,
    Richard Mears sur.
Croswell, George m. Susanna Corbin, 1785 cir. Not
    dated - Richard Drummond sur.
Crowson, John m. Nancy Kelly, 7 Jan. 1801, Benjamin
    Pruit sur.
Crowson, Levin m. Amey Powell, 2 Jan. 1795, Edmund
    Only sur.
Crowson, Major m. Nancy Bull, 2 Aug. 1800, Levin
    Crowson sur.
Crowson, William m. Polly Watson, 27 Dec. 1798,
    William Wise sur.
Cuttar, Smith m. Sabra Coleburn, 29 Aug. 1792
Custis, Henry m. Susanna Slocomb, 9 Apr. 1787,
    Southy Simpson sur.
Custis, Revel, Jr. m. Sarah Custis, 20 Dec. 1784,
    Revel Custis, Sr. sur.
Custis, Revell m. Peggy Smart Stringer, 23 Jan.
    1795 (Badly damaged)
Custis, Robinson m. Frances Yearby West, dau. John
    West 30 Nov. 1775, Edmund Custis sur.
Custis, Thomas, Jr. m. Anne Simkins, 28 Apr. 1802
Custis, Thomas m. Nancy Dis. 28 Dec. 1805, George
    Twiford sur.
Custis, William Smith m. Bridget Pennock, 2 Jan.
    1787, George Oldham sur.

Davison, Derry m. Amy, a black woman, 4 Jan. 1792
Davis, Henry m. Damey Lillaston, 16 Dec. 1805,
    David Davis sur.
Davis, Joseph m. Molly Crippen, dau. of Zipporah
    Davis, 8 Sept. 1806, George Marshall sur.
Davis, William m. Betsey Gillett, 28 Jan. 1806,
    Levin Taylor sur.
Delastatus, Peter m. Mary Dickerson, 12 Jan. 1786,
    Ezekiel Delastatus sur.
Delastatius, Selby m. Elizabeth Jester, dau.
    Rachel Jester, 22 Apr. 1786, John Sharlock
    sur.
Delastatius, Sebastian m. Peggy Pratt, 1 Oct. 1790
Dickerson, Edward m. Nancy Taylor, 29 Nov. 1791
Dickerson, John T. m. Lydia Nock, 1 Oct. 1805,
    Ayres Tatham sur.

Dickerson, Michael m. Rebecca Taylor, 27 Dec. 1787

Dix, Asa m. Betsey Fletcher, 16 Nov. 1802

Dix, Levin m. Barshaby Sturges, 3 Dec. 1774, John Dix
       sur.

Dix, Richard m. Tabitha Parks, 24 July 1792

Douglas, James m. Scarbrough Broadwater, 30 Jan.
       1786, John Joynes sur.

Dowty, John m. Mary Howell, Dau. Sarah Howell, 14
       Aug. 1775, Charles Joynes sur.

Dowty, William m. Tabitha Heath, 15 Oct. 1799, John
       Savage sur.

Downing, Arthur m. Zillah Turner, 17 Feb. 1785, John
       Michael sur.

Downing, Arthur m. Catherine Howard, 13 Mar. 1789

Downing, John m. Esther Mapp, 25 Feb. 1799, David
       Bowman sur.

Downing, William m. Elizabeth Drummond, 26 Feb. 1801

Drummond, Henry m. Sophia Rodgers, 23 Nov. 1785,
       Robert Drummond sur.

Drummond, Richard m. Elizabeth Riley, 31 Jan. 1784,
       Edmund Custis sur.

Drummond, Richard m. Esther Snead, 22 Oct. 1785,
       Edmund Custis sur.

Drummond, Richard m. Nancy Fletcher, 11 Jan. 1801
       Edmund Bayly sur.

Drummond, Robert m. Peggy Drummond, 5 Nov. 1801
       Richard Drummond sur.

Drummond, Stephen m. Catherin Trader, 6 May 1794

Drummond, William, Jr. m. Anne Robinson Smith, dau.
       William R. Smith, 4 Jan. 1775, Tully Robinson
       Wise sur.

Drummond, William, Jr. m. Anne Robinson Riley, 14
       Apr. 1786, William Gibb sur.

Dunton, William m. Mary Coleburn 21 Dec. 1798,
       George Coleburn sur.

Duncan, ------m. Fanney Marshall (About 1790-99-
       Badly damaged)

Duncan, James, widower, m. Anne Hoor, widow, 18
       Dec. 1790, Southy Bull sur. (Badly damaged)

Duncan, James m. Nancy Dix, 12 Oct. 1799, John A.
       Bundick sur.

E-------, John m. Tabith Vessels ---- 1794
       (Badly damaged)

Edmunds, William m. Peggy Satchell Wyatt, 7 July
    1799, John Edmunds sur.
Edwards, Zorobable m. Jenny Hanniford, 19 Dec. 1805,
    Nathaniel Badger sur.
Eichelberger, James m. Susan Finney, dau. Euphamey
    Finney, 28 May 1806, William White Burton
    sur.
Elliott, William m. Elizabeth Fisher, 18 Mar. 1806,
    Phillip Fisher sur.
Eson, George, m. Sally Hall, 30 Dec. 1801, John Hall
    sur.
Eshon - Eson - Eshom - Isham
Evans, Arthur m. Jenny Handy, 11 Sept. 1798, George
    Matthews sur.
Evans, Crippen m. Scarbrough Davis, 7 Nov. 1805,
    William Ardis sur.
Evans, George Crippen m. Leah Brumbley, 1 Aug. 1793
    (Badly damaged)
Evans, Henry m. Polly Powell, wid. 23 Dec. 1800,
    James Rooks sur.
Evans, Jacob m. Peggy White, 23 Sept. 1790
Evans, John m. Lucretia Watson, 23 July 1785,
    Southy Simpson sur.
Evans, John m. Leah Robins, 25 Feb. 1793, George
    Mathews sur.
Evans, John, son of Francis, m. Polly Parks 24
    June 1806, Severn Tyler sur.
Evans, Levin m. Rebecca Mathews, 17 May 1785, John
    Derby sur.
Evans, Levin m. Sarah Thomas, 31 Aug. 1788
Evans, Robert m. Katey Daniel, 26 Mar. 1774,
    William Drummond, Sr. sur.
Evans, Thomas m. Sarah Marshall, wid. 20 July
    1801
Evans, William m. Jenney Melvin, 15 Oct. 1799,
    Elisha Whealton sur.
Ewart, Robert m. Margaret Boggs, 15 Feb. 1787,
    George Smith sur.
Ewell, Charles m. Sally Schoolfield, 4 Oct. 1788
Ewell, George m. Amey Bloxom, 30 Dec. 1805, Elias
    Taylor sur.
Ewell, James m. Esther Whealton, 26 Mar. 1788
Ewell, James m. Rachel Parks, 2 Oct. 1789
Ewell, Solomon m. Polly Justice, 4 Jan. 1792

Ewell, William Whittington m. Anne Mathews, 7 Oct.
    1783, Charles Ewell sur.

Finney, John, Jr. m. Nancy Broadwater, 28 July 1794
Finney, John m. Catherine B------man, 2 Sept. 1799,
    William Seymour sur. (Badly damaged)
Finney, William m. Elizabeth S. Marshall, 31 Jan.
    1787, Thomas Evans sur.
Finney, William m. Sally Bundick, 5 Oct. 1801,
    Edmund Bayly sur.
Fisher, Maddox m. Leah Mears, 15 Jan. 1802, John
    Justice sur.
Fisher, Teackle m. Nancy Johnson, 23 May 1792
Fischer, William m. Elizabeth Rodgers, wid. 3 Nov.
    1774, John Finney sur.
Fitchett, John m. Joyce Andrews, 21 Jan. 1786,
    Griffin Savage sur.
Fletcher, Stephen m. Bekey Wyatt, 26 Nov. 1804,
    William T. Barcraft sur.
Fletcher, Thomas m. Elizabeth Choard, 9 Aug. 1804,
    John Wallop sur.
Floyd, Benjamin m. Sarah Hornsby, 8 June 1794
Floyd, Frederick m. Sarah Bayly, 17 Sept. 1804,
    Jonathan Garrison sur.
Floyd, James m. Catherine Kellam, 28 Dec. 1785,
    Charles Richardson sur.
Foster, Abraham m. Charity Bagge, 21 Feb. 1786,
    William Gibb sur.
Foster, Selby m. Nancy Foster, 14 June 1806
Fosque, John m. Margaret Custis, 3 July 1786,
    Francis Savage sur.
Fosque, William m. Leah Dickerson, 3 Feb. 1786,
    Edward Dickerson sur.
Freeman, Robert m. Esther Carter, 12 Oct. 1790
Furness, Ephraim m. Polly Massey, 7 Jan. 1799,
    Isaac Henderson sur.

Garret, Charles m. Rosey Chandler, 5 Sept. 1798,
    Edward Ironmonger sur.
Garrett, John m. Salley Taylor, 28 Mar. 1787,
    George Trewet Taylor sur.
Garrison, Edmund m. Adah Fletcher, 7 Nov. 1806,
    Samuel Garrison sur.
Garrison, Isaiah m. Adah Churen, 6 Aug. 1783,
    Berry Floyd sur.

Garrison, Samuel m. Elizabeth Groten, 2 Aug. 1804,
     Benjamin Harrison sur.

Gaskins, Teackle m. Mary Riggs, dau. Joshua Riggs,
     11 July 1806, Arthur Watson and George
     Eshon sur.

Gascoynes, William m. Esther Mathews, 27 June 1796

George, freed by Bagwell, m. Scarburgh Tunnill,
     free negro, 13 Aug.1800, Daniel sur.

George, a negro man m. Milly a free negro woman
     29 Dec. 1806, Samuel Downing sur.

Giddens, Reuben m. Betsy Vessells, 20 Dec. 1797

Gillett, John m. Mary Wallop, 8 Sept. 1791

Gilchrist, Andrew m. Laney Middleton, 15, Apr. 1805
     Richard D. Bayly sur.

Gladding, John m. Hepsey Powell, 10 Jan. 1800,
     William Delastatius sur.

Godwin, Esau m. Ann S. West, 8 Feb. 1802, Jonathan
     West sur.

Godwin, Nicholas P. m. Sally Duncan, 2 Apr. 1805

Gray, Solomon m. Betsy Lewis, 27 Dec. 1791

Green, John m. Bekey Wilson, 29 Oct. 1799

Grinnalds, Southey m. Ader West, 21 Jan. 1806, Isaac
     Wright sur.

Grinales, Southy m. Sarah Abbot, 2 Aug. 1786,
     Edmund Custis sur.

Groten, Zorababel m. Anne Kellam, 29 Aug. 1785,
     Levin Walker sur.

Guy, John m. Ann Parker, 10 Sept. 1799, Henry Guy
     sur.

Guy, Major m. Rachel Milliner, 21 June 1783,
     Thomas Copes sur.

Hack, Peter, son of Peter Hack, m. Elizabeth
     Smith, dau. John Smith, 17 Nov. 1774,
     Levin Joynes sur.

Haggoman, John m. Mary Anne Jameson, 18 June 1786
     George Ker sur.

Haines, William m. Sarah Migee, 2 Jan. 1787, Jacob
     Taylor sur.

Hall, Charles m.Lucretia Moore, 1 Mar. 1786,
     George Young sur.

Hall, John m. Henrietta Dixon, 2 Sept. 1801,
     Elijah Shay sur.

Hammond, Charles m. Comfort ------ 27 Sept. 1787,
     John Burton sur.

Harrison, Savage m. Euphamy Kellam, 8 Jan. 1800,
 Jacob Kelley sur.
Harrison, William m. Mary Turlington, 6 July 1786,
 Thomas Snead sur.
Hargis, Custis m. Pricilla Pearce, 13 June 1800,
 John Pearce and Smith Bunting sur.
Hargis, Thomas m. Wise Marshall, 16 Nov. 1786, George
 Corbin sur
Harmon, John m. Mary Bird, 30 Jan. 1806, John Bird
 sur.
Harman, Zorobable m. Sally Watson, 5 Jan. 1787,
 Robert Walker sur.
Harvey, Henry m. Patience Chandler, 22 May 1806,
 Thomas Chandler sur.
Heath, Joseph m. Susanna Heath, 11 Feb. 1786, Henry
 Heath sur.
Heath, Major m. Peggy Harmon, 27 Jan. 1806, Robert
 Nock sur.
Henderson, John m. Martha Boston, 16 Oct. 1799,
 George Bonwell sur.
Henderson, James, m. Peggy Johnson, 19 Oct. 1801,
 John Johnson sur.
Henderson, Lemuel m. Catherine Beard, 23 Dec. 1805,
 Zadoc Selby sur.
Hickman, Arthur m. Betsy Parks, 16 Apr. 1800, John
 Dix sur.
Hickman, Arthur m. Betsy Only 2, Jan. 1801
Hickman, Dennis m. Bridget Dix, 2 Apr. 1892
Hickman, Edward m. Peggy Parker, 25 Aug. 1787,
 Samuel Parker sur.
Hickman, Henry m. Lissa Balye, 10 Oct. 1789
Hickman, John Berry m. Mary Pettitt, 13 Feb. 1787,
 Thomas Hickman sur.
Hickman, Richard m. Elizabeth Waterfield, 5 Jan.
 1787, Selby Hickman sur.
Hickman, Spencer m. Peggy Bayly, 31 May 1791
Hickman, Stephen m. Esther Dix, 15, Oct. 1796
Hickman, Thomas m. Delaney Lillaston, 3 June
 1735, Willett Lillaston sur.
Hinman, George m. Polly Young, 2 Dec. 1797
Hinman, Major m. Mrs. Seymour Hickman, Wid. 26
 Dec. 1798
Hinman, Moses m. Elizabeth Howard, 17 June 1799,
 Littleton Walker sur.

Hinman, William m. Tabitha Bundick, 3 Nov. 1796

Hoffman, William m. Molly Hutson, 2 Feb. 1800, George
      Wilson sur.

Holland, Thomas m. Elizabeth Selby, dau. Nancy
      Selby, 12 Jan. 1799, Thomas Cropper, Benj.
      Potter and Edmund Bayly sur.

Holston, John m. Catey Prewit, 11 May 1784, Thomas
      Snead sur.

Holmes, Thomspon m. Elizabeth A. Stockly, 29 May
      1805, Richard D. Bayly sur.

Hope, Charles m. Rachel Bell, 6 May 1786, Caleb
      Broadwater sur.

Hope, Charles m. Rachel Bell, 6 May 1786, (license)

Hopkins, Henry m. Polly Tarr, 17 Jan. 1806, David
      Watts sur.

Hornsby, Eli m. Anne Bird 24 Apr 1800, Edmund
      Hornsby sur.

Hornsby, William m. Polly Hornsby, 16 Sept. 1801,
      James Hornsby sur.

Hudson, George Gore m. Molly Shay, 2 Sept. 1789

Hunt, Thomas m. Abigail Sturges, 13 Dec. 1775,
      John Barnes sur.

Hurst, William m. Molly Colony, 3 Jan. 1796

Hurst, William m. Sally Guy, 31 Jan. 1801, William
      Lewis sur.

Hutson, Thomas m. Laney Simpson, 26 Aug. 1789

Hutchinson, Robert m. Elizabeth Walker, 31 Mar.
      1806, John Walker sur.

Hyslop, Levin m. Susey Davis, 11 Sept. 1798,
      Kendall Hyslop sur.

Ironmonger, Levin m. Sarah Chandler, 25 Dec. 1804,
      Edward Ironmonger sur.

Jacob, John m. Nancy Trader, 8 July 1798

Jacob, Richard m. Margaret Burton, 25 May 1789

James, James m. Molly Hope, 15 Jan. 1801, Selby
      Lilleston sur.

Jenkins, Custis m. Sally Corbin, 25 June 1788

Jenkins, James m. Polly Corbin, 15 Deeember 1797

Jenkinson, Robert m. Elizabeth Gascoynes, 20 June
      1786, John Smith sur.

John, free negro, m. Peggy, free negro, 22 June
      1789

Johnson, Caleb m. Peggy Henderson, 5 Apr. 1802, John
    Johnson sur.

Johnson, James m. Laney Harmon 30 Mar 1801

Johnson, John m. Elizabeth Taylor 30 Sept 1799

Johnson, John m. Polly Marshall, 31 Jan. 1801, Isaac
    Holland sur.

Johnson, John m. Polly Sharpley, 27 July 1805,
    Henry Thornton sur.

Johnson, Purnal m. Peggy Bull, 27 Aug. 1798, George
    Finney sur.

Johnson, Samuel m. Rosey Corbin, 4 Mar. 1800,
    Richard Kelly sur.

Johnson, William m. Peggy Gibb, dau. William Gibb,
    22 Mar. 1806, John Young sur

Jolliff, Richard m. Eckey Aimes, 22 Sept. 1800,
    Robert Twiford sur.

Jones, Edward m. Polly Whealton, 6 Sept. 1790

Jones, William m. Sarah Whealton, 3 Dec. 1805, John
    Jones sur.

Joyne, William m. Margaret Mears, 2 Dec. 1774, John
    Powell sur.

Joynes, John m. Attalantic Gectridge, 6 Feb. 1785,
    William Gibb sur.

Justice, Ralph m. Bridget Clemmons, 31 Jan. 1787,
    Nathaniel Beavens sur.

Justice, Richard m. Elizabeth Robinson, 22 Oct. 1789,
    James Rooks sur.

Kelly, Daniel m. Bridget Brimer, 10 Feb. 1806, John
    Madux sur.

Kelley, Richardson m. Sally Johnson, 4 Mar. 1800,
    Samuel Johnson sur.

Kellam, Abraham m. Anne Sinah Lecatte (not dated)
    Shadrack Lecatte sur.

Kellam, Custis m. Elizabeth Smith, 7 Sept. 1805,
    John Finney sur.

Kellam, Edward m. Nancy Gillispie, 12 Jan. 1802

Kellam, George m. Adah Kellam, 30 Dec. 1805, Esme
    Bayly sur.

Kellam, Howsen m. Betty Turlington, 3 May 1787,
    George Taylor sur.

Kellam, John m. Peggy Martin, 8 Feb. 1806, Smith
    Martin sur.

Kellam, John, son of John, m. Sally Savage, dau.
          Jacob, 1 Dec. 1806, Jacob Savage of Melson
          sur.
Kellam, Revel m. Leah Hornsby, 11 Jan. 1800, William
          Budd sur.
Kellam, Smith m. Molly Parker, 18 Sept. 1787, William
          Gibb sur.
Kellam, Zorobabel m. Bridget Addison, 2 Oct. 1798,
          David Bowman sur.
Kendall, John m. Fanney Gutridge, 24 Dec. 1785,
          Edward Arbuckle sur.
Kilmon, Ezekiel m. Polly Parks, 19 Mar. 1799
Kilman, Thomas m. Amey Justice, 13 Mar. 1802
          Edward Killman sur.
Killman, Edward m. Tabitha Gray, 2 Aug. 1792
Knox, Nicholas m. Barbara Marshall, 28 Dec. 1785,
          John McLane sur.
Knox, Nicholas m. Esther Fiddeman, 18 June 1799,
          Thomas Alexander sur.

Lankford, Selby m. Amey Lewis, 26 Feb. 1805
Lecato, Littleton m. Esther Bradford, 24 Nov. 1806
          Abel Bradford sur.
Lecatt, Augustine m. Elizabeth Rodgers, 14 Feb. 1795
          William Gibb sur.
Lee, Joseph m. Wooney Ranger, 26 Dec. 1787
Lewis, Absalom m. Molly Killmon, 28 Jan. 1789
Lewis, Absalom m. Rachel Ross, 28 Nov. 1805,
          William R. Custis sur.
Lewis, George m. Mary Taylor, 16 Jan. 1800, John
          Lewis sur.
Lewis, John m. Levinia Taylor, 27 Nov. 1797
Lewis, Thomas m. Sarah Clark, 29 Oct. 1787, William
          Gibb sur.
Lewis, William m. Sophia Bull, 18 Oct. 1800, Laban
          Gunter sur.
Lilleston, Edmund m. Sally Broadwater, 1 Nov.
          1797
Lillaston, Jacob m. Susanna West, 28 July 1787,
          Levin Copes sur.
Lingo, John m. Nancy Martin, 3 Dec. 1805, George
          Guy sur.
Lingo, Robinson m. Peggy White, 18 Apr. 1787,
          Kendal Richardson sur.

Lingo, Thomas m. Agnes Kellam, 13 May 1797, Thomas
    Mears sur.
Lingo, William m. Thamar Martin, 3 Dec. 1805, George
    Guy sur.
Longe, Coleburn m. Nancy Thomas, 27 Nov. 1788
Lucas, Elizjah m. Betsy Taylor, 27 Oct. 1800, Richard
    Taylor sur.
Lucas, Major m. Polly Sprungs, 31 July 1805, Zadock
    Bayly sur.
Luker, John m. Sarah Finney Read, 6 Oct. 1786, Daniel
    Richardson sur.
Lurton, Littleton m. Patience Bishop, 26 Sept. 1785,
    Babel Chandler sur.

McCready, James m. Elizabeth Marshall, 28 June 1786
    John McLane sur.
McCredy, William m. Sarah Bunting, 13 July 1804,
    John Slocomb sur.
MacMath, John m. Sally Trader, 18 June 1805, Thomas
    Custis sur.
McMath, Zadock m. Polly Copes, 28 Feb. 1792
McMaster, William m. Elizabeth Henderson, 7 Dec.
    1805, Levin Hicks Dollinor sur.
Mapp, George m. Leah Harrison, 10 Jan. 1807, Thomas
    Bradford sur.
Martin, Andrew m. Comfort Turlington, 5 Feb. 1787,
    John Savage sur.
Martin, Henry m. Susanna Derby, 28 Sept. 1787,
    Edmund Scarburgh sur.
Marshall, George m. Sally Davis, 17 Nov. 1792
Marshall, Henry m. Nasha Chase, 18 July 1795
Marshall, Isaac, a Mulatto man, m. Elizabeth Lee,
    a Mulatto woman, 6 Jan. 1800
Marshall, James m. Esther Nock, 11 Sept. 1805,
    Skinner Marshall sur.
Marshall, Jacob R. m. Margaret Warrington, 7 Jan.
    1791
Marshall, John m. Polly Cropper, 10 Dec. 1798, Levin
    Townsend sur.
Marshall, John m. Adah Marshall, 14 June 1802,
    William Cheshire sur.
Marshall, Levin m. Esther Dennis, 29 May 1788
Marshall, Solomon m. Judah Evans, 28 June 1796
Marshall, Stephen m. Tabitha Marshall, 12 Oct. 1787
    Robert Pitt sur.

Marshall, William m. Peggy Stringer, 15 June 1784,
     William Gibb sur.
Massey, Adkins m. Mary Mathews, 9 Mar. 1790
Massey, Caleb m. Salley Thornton, 28 Apr. 1800
Mason (Mayson) Bennett m. Rachel Duncan, 11 Mar.
     1799, Solomon Johnson sur.
Mason, Bennet, ef Caleb, m. Aroda Heath, 28 Nov.
1805, William Doughty sur.
Mason, Babel m. Nancy Bull, 23 Jan. 1790
Mason, Henry m. Polly Heath 18, Jan. 1802, Edward
     Martin sur.
Mason, James m. Betty Northam, 3o June 1789
Mathews, Evans m. Elizabeth Merrill, 15 Feb. 1790
Mathews, George m. Mrs. Peggy Milburn, 24 Apr. 1797
Matthews, John, Jr. m. Sally Kellam, 22 Mar. 1799
Mathews, James m. Anne Silverthorn, 9 Feb. 1787,
     Elijah Mathews sur.
Mathews, Nathaniel m. Leah Medad, 7 Feb. 1806
Matthews, William m. Peggy Taylor, 20 Dec. 1798,
     John Taylor sur.
Mayson (Mason), Ezikiel m. Sally Matthews, 23 Jan.
     1806, Charles Smith sur.
Mears, Armstead m. Nancy Kellam, 25 Mar. 1799,
     William Joynes sur.
Mears, Arthur m. Sally Cropper Cole, 5 Nov. 1785
     Major Bayley sur.
Mears, Bartholomew m. Rebecca Bird, 31 Aug. 1795
Mears, Bartholomew m. Elizabeth Copes, 29 May
     1805, Richard Sparrow sur.
Mears, Coventon m. Nancy Roberts, 19 July 1784
     Arthur Roberts sur.
Mears, Hillary m. Uphamy Bell, 23 Sept. 1787,
     Arthur Mears sur.
Mears, Jonathan m. Leah Hyslop, 17 Oct. 1798,
     Custis Willis sur.
Mears, John m. Mrs. Nancy Phillips, 10 Feb. 1802,
     George Taylor sur.
Mears, Severn m. Nancy Waterfield, 1 Sept. 1798,
     Isaac Melson sur.
Meers, William m. Elizabeth Arlington, 6 Jan. 1806
     John Ames sur.
Mears, William, of Elisha, m Elizabeth Ashby, 15
     Nov. 1806, David Ashby sur.
Melson, Caleb m. Tabitha West, 2 May 1789

Melson, Daniel m. Amey Drummond, 24 Dec. 1785, Henry
  Fitzgerald sur.
Melson, Daniel m. Tabitha Ayres, 2 July 1794
Melson, Daniel m. Sophia Drummond, 6 Aug. 1796,
  Thomas Evans sur.
Melson, Daniel m. Betsy Wise, 9 Feb. 1801
Melson, Daniel, Sr. m. Molly Pruit, wid. John
  Pruit, 29 Jan. 1805
Melson, David, m. Nancy Fitzgerald, 25 July 1791
Melson, George m. Tabitha Kelly, 13 Mar. 1794
Melson, George m. Sarah Taylor, 23 May 1805,
  William Willett sur.
Melson, James m. Betsy Dickerson, 27 Nov. 1797
Melson, James m. Polly Dix, 28 Dec. 1797
Melson, Jeremiah m. Elizabeth Hanman, 7 Aug. 1798,
  Bennet Mason sur.
Melson, Middleton m. Rosey Mears, 25 Mar. 1797,
  Elijah Fitzgerald sur.
Melson, William m. Sally Gray, 10 Feb. 1789
Melvin, Obadiah m. Molly Dredden, 4 Aug. 1789
Merrill, Maximilian m. Mary Chapman, 30 July 1800
  Charles Stockley sur.
Merril, Thomas m. Tabitha Bunting, 11 Dec. 1798,
  Thomas Bunting sur.
Merrill, William m. Rosy Parker ---- Aug. 1790
Metcalf, Charles m. Sarah Hocke, 15 June 1775,
  Thomas Copes sur.
Metcalf, Mark m. Sarah Mathews, 1 Nov. 1783, John
  Metcalf sur.
Middleton, George m. Elizabeth Russel, 4 Jan. 1805
  William Middleton sur.
Middleton, Major m. Charity Wise, 27 Jan. 1795
Middleton, Thomas m. Rosah White, 7 Oct. 1804,
  Thomas West sur.
Miles, George m. Comfort Taylor, 9 Jan. 1790
Miles, Rodger m. Rachel Justice, 23 Dec. 1797
Milligan, John m. Sally Tunnell, 10 Mar. 1800,
  William Tunnell sur.
Milby, John m. Amey Groten, 5 July 1784
  Zorabable Groten sur.
Minson, Samuel m. Sarah Joynes, 24 Dec. 1805,
  Carvy Dunton sur.
Mister, Severn m. Keziah Evans, 2 July 1805,
  Benjamin Evans sur.

Montgomery, John m. Patience Drummond, 16 June 1775
    John Powell sur.

Mongue, Levin m. Nancy Turlington , 10 Aug. 1804,
    George Harman sur.

Moore, Bratchor m. Molly Hickman, 9 Aug. 1790

Moore, John m. Elizabeth Kilman, 20 Dec. 1797

Moore, Laban m. Mary Lankford, 3 July 1792

Moore, Levi m. Elizabeth Smith, 24 Dec. 1805,
    Stephen Moore sur.

Morris, Gilbert m. Elizabeth Richardson --26 1805

Morrison, John m. Comfort Potter, 4 Dec. 1805, James
    Ironmonger sur.

Morgan, Ayres m. Fanny Bloxom, 12 Jan. 1799,
    Coventon Broadwater sur.

Nedab, Levin m. Comfort Nedab, 2 Apr. 1790

Nelson, George m. Delancy Vessels, 23 Mar. 1797

Nelson, George m. Betsy Melson, 8 Nov. 1798, Asa
    Shield sur.

Nelson, James m. Delilah Prescoat, 9 Oct. 1801

Nelson, William m. Ann Mason, 31 Dec. 1805, Jacob
    Edwards sur.

Nicholson, John m. Elizabeth Whittington, dau.
    Southy Whittington, 1 Feb. 1775,
    Sebastian Cropper, Jr. sur.

Nock, Elijah m. Lydia Hope dau. Rachel Broadwater
    22 Nov. 1798, John Nock sur.

Nock, George m. Margaret Guy, 8 Dec. 1784, Robert
    Nock sur.

Nock, John m. Peggy Broadwater, 18 Dec. 1797

Nock, Robert m. Elizabeth Heath, 17 Feb. 1787,
    Thomas Nock sur.

Nock, William m. Bridget Bundick, 30 Nov. 1784
    William Gibb sur.

Nock, Zadock m. Elizabeth Warner (not dated -
    about 1786) John Moore sur.

Northam, Southy m. Neomy Bird, 20 Jan. 1805

Ogue, William m. Susey James, 10 Jan. 1801, Robert
    James sur.

Onions, Hezekiah m. Betsy Stockly, 31 July 1792

Onions, John m. Tabitha Young, 29 June 1790

Onions, William Selby m. Sally Bundick, 6 Dec.
    1792

Only, John m. Nancy Groten, 26 Jan. 1786, Thomas
    Bonewell sur.
Outten, Abraham m. Mary Wise, 2 Feb. 1785, Peter Hack
    sur.
Outten, Ephraim m. Susanna Leatherbury, 8 Dec. 1803,
    John O. Twyford sur.
Outten, Jacob m. Keziah Conquest, 5 Aug. 1804, James
    Justis Abbott sur.
Outten, Jacob m. Mary Hancock, 23 June 1806
Outten, Purnal m. Elizabeth Taylor, 16 July 1785,
    Joshua Taylor sur.
Outten, Purnal m. Sarah Leatherberry, 25 June 1791,
    Charles Parker sur.
Owen, John m. Anne Taylor, 20 Dec. 1797
Owen, Taylor m. Scarburgh Taylor, 2 Oct. 1789

Padget, Nathaniel m. Peggy Connah, 30 July 1788
Parramore, Thomas m. Anne Hack, 25 Aug. 1786, Peter
    Hack sur.
Parramore, William, Jr. m. Margaret Teackle, 27 June
    1796
Parks, Benjamin m. Betsy Savage, 16 Sept. 1797
Parks, Edmund m. Peggy Bird, 24 Dec. 1798
Parks, Robert m. Nancy Holsten, 22 Mar. 1806
Parks, Reuben m. Pricilla Croswell, 18 Sept. 1805,
    Peter Parker sur.
Parker, John m. Sarah Simpson, dau. Southy Simpson
    31 July 1775, John Riley sur.
Parker, John, Jr. m. Mary Twiford, 2 Jan. 1790
Parker, John m. Molly Grinalds, 14 Dec. 1790
Parker, John, son of John, m. Nany Dix, 22 Dec. 1801,
    John Burton sur.
Parker, James m. Nancy East, 21 Dec. 1805, Parker
    East sur.
Parker, Samuel m. Anne Celly (Kelly?) Not dated -
    about 1787, Jacob Savage sur.
Patterson, Anderson m. Elizabeth Mills, 29 Dec. 18--
    Arthur Hickman sur (Damaged)
Paul, Jacob m. Sophia Linton, 22 Sept. 1797
Peck, Samuel m. Polly Abbott, 24 Nov. 1791
Pettitt, George m. Grace Litchfield, 10 Jan. 1801
Pettitt, Revel m. Elizabeth Baker, 3 July 1800,
    Southy Litchfield sur.

Pettitt, Thomas m. Nancy Groten, 24 Aug. 1804, George
    Pettitt sur.

Phillips, Abel m. Sally Dolby, 27 Jan. 1806, William
    Churn sur.

Phillips, Charles m. Leah Savage, 3 Jan. 1806, Francis
    Boggs, Jr. sur.

Phillips, Edward m. Nancy Smith, 14 Jan. 1799, Matthew
    Phillips sur.

Phillips, George m. Betty Powell, 31 May 1799,
    George Taylor sur.

Phillips, John m. Nancy Edmunds, 19 Aug. 1786, Thomas
    Willet sur.

Phillips, Matthias m. Nancy Melson, 28 Feb. 1799,
    John Satchell sur.

Phillips, Thomas m. Nancy Vernelson --- Feb. 1795,
    James Hanneford sur. (Badly damaged)

Phillips, William m. Mrs. Betsy Picket, 29 Sept. 1800,
    George Taylor sur.

Pigott, Jechomah m. Molly Lawrence, 14 Sept. 1787,
    William Gibb sur.

Pilchard, John m. Elizabeth Taylor, 20 Nov. 1800,
    Southy Lucas sur.

Pool, Charles m. Betsy Drummond, 9 Oct. 1804

Potter, Laban m. Sophia Spiers, 18 Aug. 1786, Benj.
    Hayley sur.

Poulson, John m. Polly Dix, 1 Dec. 1785, William
    Gibb sur.

Poulson, Zadock m. Molly Edwards, 10 Aug. 1805,
    Zerobabel Edwards sur.

Powell, Isaac m. Polly Gootee, 20 June 1792

Powell, Laban m. Mary Rew, 23 Aug. 1792

Powell, Nathaniel m. Leah Lewis, 17 Dec. 1804, John
    West sur.

Powell, Nicholas m. Elizabeth West, 22 May 1792

Powell, Nathan m. Catherine Watson, 30 Dec. 1800,
    Littleton Trader sur.

Powell, William m. Caty Lewis, 16 Apr. 1806, William
    Lewis sur.

Pruit, Benjamin m. Ritter Melson, 16 Nov. 1796

Prewit, John m. Molly Parker, 8 Nov. 1798

Read, George m. Esther Arbuckle, 14 Oct. 1805,
    Joseph Doughty sur.

Read, Revell m. Esther Taylor, 27 Feb. 1800

Read, Richard m. Jenny Bradford, 10 Mar. 1786, Edmd.
Read sur.

Read, Solomon m. Sarah Wyatt, wid. 11 Feb. 1775,
James Broughton sur.

Read, Severn m. Anne Bagge, Jr. 15, Oct. 1785, Henry
Townsend sur.

Reid, William m. Tabitha Mister, 21 Jan. 1784,
Edmund Reid sur.

Revell, John m. Elizabeth Poulson, 28 Feb. 1787;
William Gibb sur.

Revell, John K. m. Eliza S. Robins, 26 June 1805,
George Burton sur.

Rew, Charles m. Comfort Hickman, 23 Oct. 1790

Rew, Reuben m. Leah Riggs, 6 Jan. 1792

Rew, Southy m. Nanny Taylor, 28 June 1786; Smith
Melson sur.

Riggen, John m. Polly Garrett, 30 Mar. 1790

Riley, George m. Fanny West, 2 Feb. 1802, William
Riley sur.

Riley, William m. Nancy Riley, 24 Feb. 1806, Thomas
Riley sur.

Roan, Daniel m. Ader Morris, 8 Jan. 1806, Levin
Godfree sur.

Roan, Stephen m. Esther Becket, 28 Aug. 1805, Jacob
Morris sur.

Robins, John m. Susanna Teackle, 31 Mar. 1786, John
Boisnard sur.

Robinson, Thomas, Jr. m. Mrs. Nancy Turpin, 8 May
1805, Robert Twiford sur.

Roberts, Charles m. Tabitha Churn, 15 Sept. 1787,
William Gibb sur.

Roberts, Francis m. Betsy Whorton, 13 Mar. 1802,
John Roberts sur.

Roberts, Francis m. Betsy Bradford 24, Feb. 1806,
Arthur Roberts sur.

Roberts, John m. Nancy Read, wid. Severn Read
27 Oct. 1806, Jonathan Mears sur.

Rodgers, Finly m. Amey Twiford, 26 July 1786, John
Warrington sur.

Rodgers, John m. Rosanna Moore, 27 Apr. 1785, Thomas
Parker sur.

Rodgers, Levin m. Elizabeth Reid, 1 Apr. 1783,
Thomas Coleburn sur.

Rodgers, Richard m. Polly Marshall, 12 Dec. 1798,
        John Marshall sur.
Rodgers, Richard m. Betsy Collins, dau. James
        Collins, 29 Aug. 1801, Peter Delastatius
        sur.
Rodgers, Robert m. Tabitha Bundick, dau. Justic
        Bundick, 31 Oct. 1775, John Smith sur.
Rodgers, Thomas m. Nancy Cullor, 30 May 1785, Smith
        Culler sur.
Roles, John m. Susanna West, 24 Mar. 1785, William
        Gibb sur.
Roley, William m. Hepsey Silverthorne, 25 July 1798
        Robert Twiford sur.
Rooks, James m Peggy Hinman, 22 June 1799
Rooks, Thomas m. Mary Watson, 17 July 1805, Caleb
        Watson sur.
Ross, Ezekiel m. Esther Harman, 25 Oct. 1789
Ross, William m. Sally Taylor, 25 July 1800, John
        Thornton sur.
Ross, William m. Molly Hornsby, 6 Feb. 1806, Thomas
        Edmunds sur.
Russell, Abel m. Leah Chambers, 24 Mar. 1785, Gilbert
        Pielee sur.
Russell, Andrew m. Esther Bell, 28 Apr. 1800,
        Richard Sparrow sur.
Russell, Joshua m. Jane Thornton (not dated) about
        1790
Russell, Robert m. Comfort Parks, 5 Mar. 1790
Russell Solomon m. Jemimah Flewhart, 6 Aug. 1805,
        Charles Booth sur.

Salisberry, Thomas m. Sally Topping, 26 Nov. 1791
Sanford, James m. Sarah Roberts, 6 July 1774, Severn
        Guthrey sur.
Sanders, Samuel m. Keziah Hinmon, 29 May 1792
Satchell, Christopher m. Anne Bell, 28 Feb. 1786,
        William Gibb sur.
Satchell, John m. Leah Drummond, 18 Nov. 1801, James
        Snead sur.
Saunders, Thomas m. Elizabeth Brimer, 22 Dec. 1789
Savage, Jacob m. Mary Kellam, 6 June 1786,
        Zorabable Chandler sur.
Savage, Joseph m. Peggy Sturgis, 9 Dec. 1799, Arthur
        Savage sur.

Savage, Robert m. Nancy Kellam, 29 Dec. 1801, James
    Ailworth sur.

Savage, Robinson m. Betsy Mears, 28 Aug. 1792

Savage, Richard R. m. Mrs. Elizabeth Broadwater,
    7 July 1806, Smith Cutler sur.

Savage, Zerobabel m. Molly James, 1 Sept. 1804,
    Savage Crippen sur.

Scott, George m. Betsey Ewell, 5 Jan. 1801, Mark
    Ewell sur.

Selby, George m. Polly Custis, 18 Sept. 1800, Arthur
    White sur.

Shay, Eli m. Agnes Trader, 12 Nov. 1788

Sharply, John m. Sally Cary, 23 Mar. 1801, Levin
    Taylor sur.

Sharply, William m. Esther Whealton, 15 Jan. 1799,
    Beverly Copes sur.

Sharwood, William m. Mrs. Peggy Allen, 14 Apr. 1802,
    Edmund Bayly sur.

Sharrod, George m. Molly K. Godwin, 4 Mar. 1805

Sharrod, Thomas m. Elizabeth Mister, 6 Apr. 1805,
    John Sharrod sur.

Shield, John m. Mary Barnes, 17 Oct. 1801, Spencer
    Barnes sur.

Shrieves, Teackle m. Molly Middleton, 3 Sept. 1798,
    George Middleton sur.

Silverthorn, Burton m. Susanna Dunton, 12 Dec. 1800,
    William Wyatt sur.

Silverthorn, William m. Levinia Corbin, 21 Oct. 1796

Simpson, Elijah m. Betsy Beasly, 30 Jan. 1802,
    Zerobabel Budd sur.

Simpson, George m. Leah Melson, 28 May 1801,
    William Kelley sur.

Simpson, Hancock m. Anne Barnes, 27 Jan. 1786,
    Richard Drummond, Jr. sur.

Simpson, John m. Nancy West, 24 Feb. 1784, Charles
    West sur.

Simpson, Southy m. Hannah Rodgers, 2 June 1786,
    William Gibb sur.

Singleton, Richard m. Esther Shreaves, 26 Mar. 1790

Slover, John m. Peggy Twiford, 26 Dec. 1805, Selby
    Foster sur.

Slocomb, William m. Anne Banister, 31 Oct. 1797

Small, Robert m. Hepsey Johnson, 27 Aug. 1804

Smart, Henry m. Sally Hoffman, 26 Nov. 1806, Andrew
    Hoffman sur.

Smart, Nathaniel m. Nancy Bunting, 18 Nov. 1784,
 William Bunting sur.
Smith, Elisha m. Nancy Wheatly, 29 June 1804, Levin
 Mathews sur.
Smith, George m. Ruth Parker, 24 Dec. 1798, Edward
 Phillips sur.
Smith, Isaac m. Margaret Dowty, 15 June 1802, David
 Bowman sur.
Smith, James m. Mary Jackson, 22 Jan. 1787, Ezekiel
 Delastatius sur.
Smith, Ralph m. Scarburgh Whealton, 29 June 1787,
 Valentine Smith sur.
Smith, Solomon m. Betsey Outten, 12 Sept. 1786,
 Robert Twiford sur.
Smulling, ----- m. Nancy Delastatius, 25 Mar. 1799,
 William Brewington sur.
Snead, Bowdoin m. Polly Kellam, 29 Apr. 1790
Snead, George m. Sarah Bayly, 14 Mar. 1790
Snead, George m. Catherine Watson, 26 Jan. 1801,
 Charles Snead sur.
Snead, George m. Elizabeth Ironmonger, 27 June, 1805
 Daniel Ardis sur.
Snead, Isaac m. Nancy Sharwood, 3 Dec. 1801, John
 Hogshire sur.
Snead, John H. m. Betsy Drummond of Robert, 9 May
 1801
Snead, John m. Milly Chandler, 26 Dec. 1798, Bowdin
 Snead sur.
Snead, James m. Susanna Satchell, 7 Aug. 1798, John
 Satchell sur.
Snead, James m. Mrs. Sally Window, 28 Oct. 1801,
 John Satchell sur.
Snead, Robert m. Esther Scott, 5 Aug. 1783, Bayly
 Hinman sur.
Snead, Thomas m. Elizabeth West, 23 May 1785,
 William Gibb sur.
Solomon, a negro man m. Tamer, a negro woman, 28
 Dec. 1798
Sparrow, Richard m. Esther Wise, 6 Oct. 1789
Sparrow, Richard m. Zeporah Mears ---- ---- 1796
Spence, Thomas, R. P. m. Margaret D. Thomas 25
 Nov. 1805, John Wallop sur.
Speight, Josiah m. Sally East, 28 Apr. 1806,
 Elijah Bloxom sur.

Speirs, William m. Nancy Hornsby, 26 Jan. 1802,
    Samuel Coleburn sur.

Staton, John m. Comfort Conquest, 30 Dec. 1805,
    Nathaniel Conquest sur.

Staton, Thomas m. Mary Kelpin, 8 Sept 1810, John
    Holt sur.

Stant, James m. Euphamy Wilson, 31 Aug. 1795

Stakes, Johannes m. Anne Parker, 27 Feb. 1799,
    William Guy sur.

Sterling, John m. Lovey Mason, 24 Dec. 1805, Jacob
    Mason sur.

Stewart, James m. Sophia Bayly, 6 Nov. 1798

Stevens, Elisha m. Sally Holston, 25 Apr. 1795

Stevens, John m. Sukey Badger, 29 Dec. 1804, Charles
    Stevens sur.

Stevens, William m. Betsy Parks, 28 Feb. 1798

Stephens, Thomas m. Betty Francis, free negro, 13
    July 1804, Babel Major, free negro, sur.

Stephens, William m. Leah Tatham, 25 Apr. 1786,
    Ezekiel Tatham sur.

Stephens, William m. Keziah Sanders, 26 June 1798

Stevenson, Jonathan m. Anne Mills, 3 Apr. 1786,
    Preeson Snead sur.

Stevenson, Thomas m. Mary T. Parker, 10 Nov. 1806,
    Robert Parker sur.

Stockley, Charles m. Margaret Allen, 29 June 1784,
    John Burton sur.

Stockley, Charles m. Anne Taylor, 15 Sept. 1788

Sturgis, John m. Tabitha Royal, 15 July 1774,
    Benjamin Royal sur.

Sturgis, John, Jr. m. Mrs. Peggy Richardson, Wid.
    4 Aug. 1801, Thomas Scarburgh sur.

Sturgis, Joshua m. Joanna Guy, 23 Oct. 1787, George
    Corbin sur.

Summers, Richard m. Elizabeth Giddens, 29 Dec. 1800,
    Ephriam Vessels sur.

Summers, Richard m. Elizabeth Ewell, 6 May 1804,
    Arthur Hickman sur.

Tatham, Rickets m. Comfort Meers, 18 Oct. 1792

Taylor, Ayres m. Rachel Copes, 28 July, 1791

Taylor, Abel m. Mrs. Elizabeth Mason, 25 Sept. 1797

Taylor, Bagwell m. Lucretia Warner, 3 Nov. 1806,
    William Warner sur.

Taylor, Charles Bayley m. Betsey Walker, 11 Apr.
    1787, John Watson sur.

Taylor, Charles m. Tabitha Miles, 18 Mar. 1793
Taylor, Charles m. Sally Shipman, 31 Dec. 1800
        George Parker sur.
Taylor, Charles m. Tabitha Parks, 4 June 1806,
        William Taylor sur.
Taylor, Ephraim m. Agnes Wilkerson, 19 Dec. 1805,
        Wilson Taylor sur.
Taylor, Edward m. Diadamia Drummond, wid, 23
        Sept. 1773, Benjamin Peck sur.
Taylor, Hezekiah m. Sally Adams, 15 June 1791
Taylor, Henry m. Esther O. Sturgis, 12 Nov. 1804,
        William W. L. Marshall sur.
Taylor, Jacob m. Elizabeth Melson, 8 July 1786,
        William Willet sur.
Taylor, John m. Rachel Nock, 11 Jan. 1799, Benjamin
        Nock sur.
Taylor, John m. Hester Staton, dau. Warrington
        Staton, 18 Jan. 1802, James Taylor sur.
Taylor, James m. Caty Moore, 19 Aug. 1800, Teackly
        Taylor sur.
Taylor, James m. Ann Bagwell, 25 Feb. 1801, James
        White sur.
Taylor, James m. Esther Boggs, 13 Feb. 1802, Joseph
        Boggs sur.
Taylor, James m. Tabitha Bundick, 1 June 1804,
        Daniel Melson sur.
Taylor, Levin m. Sophia Nelson, 25 July 1805,
        Samuel Mills sur.
Taylor, Major m. Rachel Addison, 6 Oct. 1787, Peter
        Rodgers sur.
Taylor, Mathias m. Nancy Hardy, 22 Nov. 1786, James
        Smith sur.
Taylor, Matthews m. Sally Thornton, 22 Dec. 1798,
        Thomas Beavans sur.
Taylor, Purnell m. Sally Holt, 28 Dec. 1804, John
        Madrick sur.
Taylor, Selby m. Susanna Evans, 27 Oct. 1789
Taylor, Shadrack m. Ritta Fitchette, 26 Jan. 1789
Taylor, Southy m. Peggy Rew, 14 Dec. 1797
Taylor, Stephen m. Frances Melson, 27 May 1800,
        Jonathan Melson sur.
Taylor, Teackle m. Susanna Bayly, 23 Nov. 1774,
        Elijah Watson sur.

Taylor, Teackle m. Peggy Mason, 28 Sept. 1790, James
      Taylor sur.
Taylor, Thomas Teackle m. Mrs. Nancy Williams, 27 Dec.
      1802
Taylor, William, Carpenter,m. Sally Copes, 25 Jan
      1791
Taylor, William m. Nancy Wilson, 30 July 1798, George
      Wilson sur.
Taylor, William m. Tabitha Killman, 30 June 1800,
      Charles Taylor sur.
Taylor, William m. Mrs. Ede Read, wid. 3 June 1806,
      Elias Taylor sur,
Teackle, John m. Esther Beavans, 28 ---- 1794
      (Badly damaged)
Teackle, Thomas m. Catherine Stockley, 8 Feb. 1785,
      William Gibb sur.
Thomas, George m. Elizabeth Nock, 11 Jan. 1806,
      David Davis sur.
Thomas, Joshua m. Rachel Evans, 10 Sept. 1797
Thornton, James m. Sally Cottingham, 9 Feb. 1786
Thornton, Jonathan m. Mary Owen, 5 May 1791
Thornton, Jonathan m. Sally Ross, 26 May 1806,
      James Thornton sur.
Thornton, John m. Margaret Broadwater, 27 Nov. 1792
Thornton, Kendall m. Betsey Read, 20 Apr. 1796
Thornton, William m. Margaret Taylor, 19 July 1791
Tignor, Phillip m. Elizabeth Hancock, 9 June 1786,
      Severn Mears sur.
Tignal, James m. Nancy Turlington, 15 Apr. 1786,
      Nicholas Shield sur.
Topping, George m. Rosey Bonwell, 24 Dec. 1795
Topping, Garret m. Scarburgh Snead, 22 Mar. 1785,
      Tully Snead sur.
Topping, William m. Sally Wise, 26 Nov. 1791
Townsend, Covinton m. Nancy Benson, 28 May 1799
Townsend, Henry m. Sally Lurton, 17 June 1786,
      William Townsend sur.
Townsend, Joseph m. Nancy ----ey, 2 Jan. 1790
      (Badly damaged)
Townsend, Littleton P., m. Ann Blair Henry, 29
      June 1801, Thomas M. Bayly sur.
Townsend, Levin m. Hepsey Hargis, 10 Dec. 1798,
      John Marshall sur.

Trader, Arthur m. Katherine Burton, 1 Dec. 1786,
 Samuel Trader sur.

Trader, Archibald, Jr. m. Elizabeth Northam, dau.
 William Northam, 3 July 1806, Teackle Trader
 sur.

Trader, Samuel m. Patience Taylor, 19 May 1787,
 Arthur Trader sur.

Trader, Staten m. Nancy Smith, 21 Apr. 1791

Tull, George m. Polly Merril, 11 Apr. 1799, Thomas
 Slocomb sur.

Tunnell, John m. Elizabeth Ayres, 22 Feb. 1802
 Zadock Nock sur.

Tunnell, Warrington m. Rachel Clouds, 17 Jan. 1786,
 William Andrews sur.

Turlington, Aser m. Elizabeth Sturgis, 6 June, 1799,
 Robert Rodgers, Sr. sur.

Turlington, Charles m. Margaret Wimborough, 1 May
 1800, Kendall Turlington sur.

Turnal, Major m. Sally Parks, 5 Apr. 1795

Turner, Andrew m. Betsy Mathews, 26 Feb. 1806, John
 Turner sur.

Turner, John m. Mary Kellam, 27 Aug. 1799, John Bell
 sur.

Turner, John m. Sukey Evans, 30 May 1804, Major
 Shepherd sur.

Turner, Richard m. Rachel Joynes, 30 Sept. 1806,
 Stephen Pewsey sur.

Turner, Smith m. Abigail Prewit, 30 Oct. 1797

Turner, Smith m. Nancy Kellam, 9 July 1799, Arthur
 Savage sur.

Turner, William m. Caty Abbdill, 29 Sept. 1800,
 James Hornsby sur.

Twiford, Purnell m. Elizabeth Hanniford, 17 Apr. 1805
 Richard D. Bayly sur.

Twiford, Robert m. Mrs. Comfort West, 14 Mar. 1805

Twiford, Zorabable m. Agnes Watson, 5 Apr. 1786,
 James Twoford sur.

Tyler, Thomas m. Sally Hopkins, 10 Sept. 1801

Vessels, Arthur m. Betsy Bundick, 8 Jan. 1794

Vessells, John m. Vice Tull, 18 Dec. 1789

Vessels, Ephriam m. Nancy Parks, 12 Jan. 1789

Vessels, Ephriam m. Nancy Gray, 23 Feb. 1801

Vessells, William, Jr. m. Leah Northam, 13 Oct. 1798,
 George Wilson sur.

Vessels, William m. Sally Killmon, 30 Dec. 1799
Vermelson, William m. Sarah Pettitt, 17 Apr. 1806
        Parker Coard sur.

Waggoman, Joseph m. Betsey Scott Lane, 6 Jan. 1787
        Walter Bayne sur.
Walker, Levin, M. Elizabeth Peck, 12 Oct. 1785
        Isaiah Evans sur.
Walker, Southy m. Susanna Hutson, 9 Feb. 1805
Walker, William m. Betsy Bundick, 1 December 1801
        Elijah Shay sur.
Wallace, James m. Mary Warrington, 10 Nov. 1785
        James Warrington sur.
Wallop, George m. Comfort Rowly, 1 Dec. 1785, Tully
        Wise sur.
Walter, Richard m. Polly Benston, 26 Jan. 1801
        Francis Savage sur.
Walter, Thomas m. Nancy Sturgis, dau. John
        Sturgis, Sr., 27 Mar. 1802, Jacob Sturgis
        sur.
Waltham, Teackle m. Rosannah Colony, 22 Dec. 1774
        Littleton Colony sur.
Ward, Isaac m. Molly Andrews, 7 Feb. 1786, William
        Stran sur.
Warner, George m. Elizabeth West, 28 Dec. 1784
        Thomas Coverly sur.
Warren, James m. Mrs. Rebecca Langan, 6 Mar. 1798
Warrington, John m. Susanna Savage, 7 Dec. 1774
        John Powell sur.
Warrington, John m. Elizabeth Burton, 6 May 1778
        William Gibb sur.
Warrington, James m. Keziah Richardson, 26 Feb.
        1785, John Phillips, sur.
Warrington, Southy m. Euphamia Warrington, 18 Sept.
        1805, Richard Rodgers sur.
Waters, Francis m. Sally Dennis, 27 Oct. 1785, John
        Teackle sur.
Watts, Davis m. Peggy Thomas (not dated-about
        1786) John Robins Coard sur.
Watson, Arthur m. Betsy Finney, 31 July 1792
        Samuel Wilson
Watson, Benjamin T. m. Peggy Smith Garrett, 29 Nov.
        1785, Caleb Broadwater sur.
Watson, Jacob m. Nancy Biggs, 27 Apr. 1784

Watson, James Tatham m. Nancy Bloxom, 19 Feb. 1796
Watson, John m. Sally Bunting, 25 Mar. 1799, Major
        Hastings sur.
Waterfield, Isaac m. Betsey Addison, 16 Mar. 1801
        Elijah Hancock sur.
Waterfield, William m. Polly Beavans, 4 Mar. 1786
        Mathew Taylor sur.
Weldy, William m. Rhoda Joynes, 15 May 1789
Welburn, John m. Coleburn Guy, 12 Aug. 1786, William
        Gibb sur.
Welburn, William m. Sabra Corbin, 5 Feb. 1784
        Coleburn Lang sur.
Westerhouse, Reuben m. Euphamy Merrill, 2 Nov. 1785
        George Corbin sur.
West, Benjamin m. Mary Ann Vessells, 8 Sept. 1789
West, Benjamin m. Peggy Russell, 7 June 1800
        John Custis (B.S.) sur.
West, John m. Tabitha Wise, 4 Feb. 1785, John
        Sherlock sur.
West, John m. Amey Vessells, 18 Feb. 1789
West, John m. Rachel Guy, Widow, 24 June 1802,
        Edmund Bayly sur.
West, John m. Mrs. Polly Powell, 27 Dec. 1802
Wharton, Bagwell m. Esther Tunnel, 28 Dec. 1791
        1784, William Gibb sur.
Wharton, John m. Elizabeth W. Williams 6 June
        1784, William Gibb sur.
Whealton, Elisha m. Anne Ewell, 7 May 1788
Whealton, Elisha m. Amey Evans, 14 Jan. 1790
        Jeremiah Taylor sur.
Whealton, Charles m. Polly Taylor, 14 Jan. 1800
        George Matthews sur.
Whealton, Smith m. Betsey Mason, 12 Nov. 1801
Wheatley, John m. Rebecca Addison, 26 Feb. 1800
Whittington, John m. Elizabeth Drummond, 11
        Sept. 1799, Colmore Bayne sur.
White, Caleb m. Polly Lewis, 14 Oct. 1805, John
        Benson sur.
White, George m. Nancy Lewis, 29 July 1799
        Ezekiel Bloxom sur.
White, Henry m. Esther Mathews, 30 Nov. 1785
        Joseph Mathews sur.
White James m. Lacy Laws, 5 Aug. 180 .

White, Jacob m. Sally Coursey, 31 Jan. 1797
White, John m. Tabitha Whealton, 30 June 1800
      Southy Northam sur.
White, Levin m. Betsy Ardis, 11 Apr. 1799
White, Ralph m. Elizabeth Wilkerson, 25 Mar. 1805
White, Solomon m. Bridget Hickman, 20 Aug. 1789
      (Badly damaged)
White, William m. Susanna Guy, 24 Nov. 1785, Major
      Chambers sur.
White, William m. Nancy Justice, 7 Nov. 1798
      Daniel Baker sur.
William, freed by Richard Drummond m. Rachel,
      freed by William Layfield, 1 Feb. 1800
      Thomas Cropper sur.
Williams, John m. Peggy Beavans, 24 Nov. 1800
      James J. Abbott sur.
Willett, George m. Nancy Riggs, 28 Dec. 1793
Willet, John m.Mrs. Sophia Lewis, Widow
      23 Dec. 1798
Willett, Thomas m. Tabitha Phillips, 17 July 1786
      John Phillips sur.
Willett, William m. Elizabeth Stephens, 26 May
      1806
Willett, Waitman m. Sarah White, 5 Mar. 1806,
      Daniel Melson, Sr. sur.
Willis, Zorababel m. Ann Rodgers, 20 Dec. 1798
      Custis Willis sur.
Wilson, George m. Rachel Northam, 31 Oct. 1796
Wilson, Severn m. Grace Adams, 1 June 1804
      Samuel Wilson sur.
Wilson, Samuel m. Tabitha Marshall, 24 Apr. 1797
Wimbrough, George m. Nancy Harman, 31 Dec.1804
Wimbrough, Richard m. Santer Hickman, 10 Mar. 1786
      John Glasby sur.
Winters, John m. Margaret Savage, 9 Dec. 1786
      Andrew Martin sur.
Wise, George m. B------ Badger ---- Dec. 1794
      William Finney sur. (Badly damaged)
Wooldridge, James m. Mary Beavans, 4 Feb. 1806
      Major Davis sur.
Wright, George m. Sally Dix, 3 Oct. 1789
Wright, Isaac m. Mary Satchell, 27 Dec. 1804
      William H. Coxon sur.

Wright, Jacob m. Rachel Pettitt, 19 June 1788
Wright, William m. Patience Dix, 28 Feb. 1797

Young, Bagwell m. Betsy Moore, 28 July 1800, Eli
      Shay sur.
Young, John m. Betty Justice, 22 Sept. 1787, James
      Vessels sur.
Young, Robert m. Rachel Rew, 22 Jan. 1800, Woney
      Rew sur.
Young, Richard m. Sally Adams, 29 Dec. 1805 John
      Young sur.
Young, Thomas m. Elizabeth Parker, dau. John R.
      Parker, 27 Nov. 1805, James Eichelberrgher
      sur.
Young, William, Jr. m. Elizabeth Crippen, 28 Nov.
      1775, Thomas Crippen sur.

-----aker m. Sophia Baker, 14 Aug. 1796
      (Badly Damaged)